Weltkulturerbe
GOSLAR

Dr. Ursula Müller

D1501288

Studio Volker Schadach, Goslar

Die Altstadt Goslar vor den Harzbergen. Im Hintergrund der 1142 m hohe Brocken.

The Old Town of Goslar at the foot of the Harz mountains. In the background the Brocken peak, elevation 1142 m.

Einleitung

Berg und Stadt sind Weltkulturerbe

Wie luftige Ausrufezeichen markieren Drachenflieger und Paraglider den "Schicksalsberg". Der Rammelsberg, die mit Gold, Silber, Blei, Zink, und Kupfer gefüllte Schatztruhe der Kaiser und Bürger, war Basis für Goslars mittelalterliche Stadtgestalt und Barometer städtischen Wohlstandes.

Sie ermöglichte den Aufstieg der Stadt zu einem kaiserlichen Tagungszentrum mit der Kaiserpfalz als Mittelpunkt und verlieh ihr den Rang einer Großstadt mit 5000 Einwohnern im 12. Jahrhundert. Aus ihren Metallen wurden die Lehnen des Kaiserstuhls (11.Jh.), die Schalen des Marktbrunnens gegossen und die Otto-Adelheid-Pfennige geprägt, die der "Euro" des Mittelalters waren.

"Schicksalsberg" auch heute noch, obwohl 1988 die Schatzkammer leergeräumt war. Im Jahr 1992 wurde das über 1000 Jahre in Betrieb befindliche Erzbergwerk Rammelsberg zusammen mit der

Introduction

Mountain and city are recognised as a world cultural heritage. And like floating exclamation marks, the hang- and para-gliders are drifting about the "Mountain of Fate". For the Rammelsberg, this treasure chest of emperor and citizens alike, once filled with gold, silver, lead, zinc, and copper, was the foundation of the medieval city and a constant measure of its wealth.

It made Goslar an imperial centre with a magnificent palace, and with some 5.000 inhabitants in the 12th century it gave the city an almost metropolitan air. The ore from its mines provided the metal for the armrests of the throne (11th century), and for the basins of the market fountain. And last but not least the mint turned out the famous Otto-Adelheid-Penny, in a way an "Euro" of the Middle Ages.

And even though that treasure chest was emptied for good in 1988, the Rammelsberg has remained Goslar's "Mountain of Fate": For in 1992 the mines, active for over a thousand years, and the historic old city were entered into the UNESCO list of

Bürgerliches Selbstbewußtsein verrät der Adler auf dem Marktbrunnen mit den größten romanischen Brunnenschalen diesseits der Alpen.

A sign of the citizens' self-confidence, the eagle sits proudly on top of the market fountain, which features the largest Romanesque basins this side of the Alps.

Dreiklang von Kaisermacht, geistlichem Fundament und bürgerlicher Selbstbehauptung: Pfalz, Marktkirche, Teufelsturm.

The triad of imperial might, spiritual foundation, and civil self-assertion: the Palace, the Market Church, and the Teufelsturm (Devil's Tower).

historischen Altstadt Goslar in die Liste des UNESCO-Weltkulturerbes aufgenommen. Es war das erste deutsche Industriedenkmal, das in diesen weltweiten Gotha der Denkmäler Eingang fand. Als Paradebeispiel für das Motto der Weltausstellung "Mensch - Natur - Technik" avancierte der Rammelsberg auch zum dezentralen Projekt der Expo 2000 in Hannover. Griffiger Titel "Expo on the rocks". Und immer dabei die Goslarer Altstadt.

Im Besucherbergwerk kann man heute hautnah den jahrhundertealten Bergbau nacherleben so wie jeder, der über das holprige Pflaster der verwinkelten Gassen in der Innenstadt spaziert, mit der Geschichte auf Du und Du steht, der kaiserlichen wie der bürgerlichen.

Ein gütiges Schicksal hat das 922 gegründete Goslar im Zweiten Weltkrieg vor der Zerstörung bewahrt. Zwar fraß der Rote Hahn wieder und wieder Lücken in die Häuserreihen, aber 168 Gebäude aus der Zeit vor 1550 - insgesamt 1000 vor 1850 - widerstanden Krieg und Feuer und werden heute noch bewohnt! Daß Schmalhans

world cultural heritage sites. It was the first German industrial monument that found its way into this "Who's Who" of historical monuments. Reflecting the World Fair's motto "Man - Nature - Technology" at its best, the Rammelsberg has also been chosen as a special site of the Expo 2000 at Hanover. The fitting slogan: "Expo on the rocks". And Goslar's Old Town is right along once again.

In the still expanding show' mine you meet centuries of mining, just as the cobbled streets and crooked lanes of the Old Town put you face to face with the imperial history as well as the past of the common citizen.

Founded in 922, Goslar was spared from the destruction of World War II by a kind fate. And while fires ravaged the city at times, 168 houses built before 1550, and a total of 1.000 built before 1850, have survived fires and wars to be still lived in today, a strange prize of poorer days that forced citizens to repair and maintain their houses rather than to build anew.

Goslar's charm comes from that unique mix of humble

Der Marktplatz ist heute Schauplatz des alltäglichen Wochenmarktes, wie auch der Märkte zu Walpurgis, zu Weihnachten und zum Altstadtfest.

The marketplace today is the scene of the weekly market as much as that of the Walpurgis and Christmas markets and the Old Town Fair.

Wie ein grünes Schaltuch umschmeicheln bewaldete Berge die tausendjährige Stadt.

Like a shawl of green the forested mountains caress the thousand-year-old city.

jahrhundertelang Küchenmeister in Goslar war, hat sich ausgezahlt, weil die Bürger dadurch gezwungen waren, ihre alten Häuschen auszuflicken und zu erhalten.

Goslars Charme erwächst aus dem Miteinander von bescheidenen oder auch aufwendigeren Bürgerhäusern und den Baudenkmälern von hohem Rang. Die Elite der letzteren ist ein Trio, das sich im Glanz der Etikette "Kulturdenkmäler von besonderer nationaler Bedeutung" sonnen darf: Kaiserpfalz, Großes Heiliges Kreuz und Breites Tor. Kein Wunder daß jährlich knapp zwei Millionen Touristen eine Stadt aufsuchen, deren Ensemble nicht nur auf Traditionsinseln reduziert ist.

Tausend Jahre sind in Goslar eine gängige Einheit, und trotzdem ist die Innenstadt keineswegs ein Museum. Moderne Skulpturen mitten in der Altstadt bilden die Brücke zwischen dem kulturellen Erbe von einst und dem Jetzt, aber auch notwendig werdende Neubauten dokumentieren den Gestaltungswillen unserer Zeit und verlieren sich nicht im Historismus.

and more prosperous houses and architectural masterpieces. A marked "cultural heritage of national importance" among them are the Kaiserpfalz, the Großes Heiliges Kreuz, and the Breites Tor, drawing almost two million visitors to this city each year, a city not reduced to some islands of tradition.

A millennium is a common measure for Goslar, and yet, the old city is not a museum. Modern sculptures right in the middle of town are bridging the gap between the cultural heritage and now, just as the necessary new buildings are a living document to the pride of today and the will to shape a future beyond a historicism.

Die Abzucht auf der Kunstmeile zwischen Museum und Stubengalerie - ein "Sprößling" der früher für das Trinkwasser zuständigen und im Stadtgebiet kanalisierten Gose.

The "mile of art" at the Abzucht between the city museum and the Stuben Gallery. Its waters are an offspring of the Gose, which once ran through underground channels and supplied the city's drinking water.

Frühlingszauber am mächtigen Flankierungsturm des Breiten Tores (um 1500).

The magic of spring transforms the mighty flanking tower of the Breites Tor.

Die im Jahr 1186 geweihte Neuwerkkirche ist die einzige Goslarer Kirche, die stilrein romanisch erhalten blieb. Neuwerk wurde nach dem Vorbild des Goslarer Doms erbaut, Ausdruck geistlicher Macht.

Consecrated in 1186, the Neuwerk Church is Goslar's only church of purely Romanesque style. Modelled after Goslar's cathedral, it was a living sign of religious might.

Seite 12/13
Die Kaiserpfalz mit dem Reichssaal im Mittelbau und der Ulrichskapelle links.

page 12/13
The Imperial Palace with the Imperial Hall at the middle and the St Ulrich's Chapel to the left.

Die spätgeborenen und dann in die Nischen der „Kaiserworth" (1494) gesetzten Kaiser verglich Heinrich Heine respektlos mit „gebratenen Universitätspedellen".

Statues of emperors, born late and then moved to their niches at the "Kaiserworth" (1494), once were likened to "roasted university janitors" by an irreverent Heinrich Heine.

Im Sauseschritt durch die Geschichte

Heinrich I. (919–936) ist der Ahnherr der Stadtgeschichte, gründete er doch 922 die Marktsiedlung Goslar. Reichsweite Bedeutung freilich erlangte dieser „vicus Goslariae" erst unter seinem Sohn, Otto I. (936–973), in dessen Regierungszeit der Erzabbau 968 im Rammelsberg begann. Die weitsichtigen Kaiser verlegten daraufhin ihre Pfalz von Werla bei Schladen nach Goslar, und Kaiser Heinrich II. (1002–1024) tat im Jahr 1005 den ersten Spatenstich für den Bau einer Pfalz. Sie erhielt unter Kaiser Heinrich III. (1039–1056) genau wie der um 1820 abgebrochene „Dom" ihre großartige Gestalt.
Zweieinhalb Jahrhunderte wurde in diesem von den „Wanderkaisern" bevorzugten Regierungssitz Reichsgeschichte geschrieben.

Das Herz Heinrichs III. ruht in der Ulrichskapelle der Pfalz, sein Körper in Speyer. Der gebürtige Goslarer Kaiser Heinrich IV. (1056–1106) trat von hier aus seinen Gang nach Canossa an.

A Shortcut to History

It all began with Heinrich (Henry) I., for he founded the small town and market place of Goslar in 922. Yet it was during the reign of Heinrich's son Otto I (936–973) that this "vicus Goslariae" began to achieve renown when the mining of ore began at the Rammelsberg in 968. Politically far-sighted, the emperors moved their seat from Werla near Schladen to Goslar, and in 1005 Emperor Heinrich II. (1002–1024) laid the foundations for a palace, which was completed in the days of Emperor Heinrich III. (1039–1056). It followed the same architectural design as the cathedral built opposite it and later demolished in 1820.

Favoured by the "travelling emperors" of the time, the Reich's history was chiefly determined at this palace for almost two and a half centuries.

As provided in his last will and testament, the heart of Heinrich III. lies at the St. Ulrich's chapel of the palace while his body rests at Speyer. And it is from his birthplace Goslar, that Emperor Heinrich

Wie ein erratischer Block ragt am Hang des Petersberges die Sandsteinklippe der Klus auf, in vorgeschichtlicher Zeit vielleicht ein Heiligtum, um 1167 eine Eremitenklause, heute eine kleine Kapelle.

The sandstone rock of the "Klus" towers like an erratic block at the side of the Petersberg. Perhaps a sacred spot of prehistoric days and a hermit's abode around 1167, it is a small chapel today.

Das Herz Kaiser Heinrichs III. ruht in einem vergoldeten Oktogon unter der Grabplatte in der Ulbrichskapelle der Kaiserpfalz. Beim Abbruch des Doms 1820 war es mehr oder minder durch Zufall noch rechtzeitig entdeckt worden. Der Körper des Saliers wurde in Speyer beigesetzt.

The heart of Emperor Heinrich III. rests in a gilded octagon under a memorial slab at the St. Ulrich's Chapel. When the cathedral was demolished in 1820, it was discovered just in time, more by chance than on purpose. The body of this Salian emperor lies at Speyer.

Goslar und sein Rammelsberg wurden zum Zankapfel zwischen Staufern und Welfen. So forderte 1176 Heinrich der Löwe den Rammelsberg als Gegengabe für eine Beteiligung an Barbarossas Italienfeldzug. In der Folgezeit führte seine Verweigerung schließlich zur Ladung vor das Reichsgericht in Goslar und zu seiner Ächtung.

Als sich die Kaiser verstärkt nach Süden wandten, verlor Goslar seine Bedeutung als heimliche Hauptstadt des Reiches. Das war die Stunde seiner Bürger, die zentrale neue Rechte erwarben und sie ausbauten. Von 1250 bis 1552 erlebte das bürgerliche Goslar seine Blütezeit, wie man noch heute an seiner Stadtgestalt ablesen kann. Bereits 1219 hatte die Stadt wichtige Privilegien von Kaiser Friedrich II. (1212–1250) erhalten. Dann kamen Schlag auf Schlag hinzu die Mitgliedschaft im Städtebund der Hanse (1268) und der Erwerb der Reichsvogtei (1290). Die Verleihung des Heerschildrechts (1340) war die Geburtsstunde der Freien Reichsstadt, die Goslar bis 1802 blieb.

Im Bergbau gab es eine wirtschaftliche Durststrecke, als

IV. (1056–1106) set out for his famous journey of penance to Canossa.

Goslar and the Rammelsberg became a bone of contention between the [imperial] Hohenstaufen and the Welfen dynasties. In 1176, the Welfen Duke Heinrich der Löwe (Henry the Lion) demanded the Rammelsberg as a gift in exchange for his participation in Emperor Friedrich Barbarossa's (Frederick I of the Holy Roman Empire) Italian campaign. Continuing to decline service, Heinrich eventually was brought before the Imperial Court at Goslar and made an outlaw.

As the emperors' interests moved southward, Goslar lost its role as the secret capital of the empire. This was the hour of Goslar's burghers, who acquired and extended new rights and privileges. Goslar today still mirrors these heydays between 1250 and 1552. Having received important privileges from Emperor Friedrich II (1212–1250) in 1219, the town became a member of the Hanseatic League in 1268, and in 1290 it was granted the protectorate over the surrounding imperial land. With the right to have

zwischen 1360 und 1460 die Grubenbaue absoffen und erst neue Technologien zu ihrer Trockenlegung entwickelt werden mußten. Ab 1460 sprudelte der Reichtum wieder, aber die Machtentfaltung Goslars weckte die Begehrlichkeit der Braunschweiger Herzöge, die die Pfandsumme für den Rammelsberg abgelöst hatten. So kam es 1552 zu einer der schwärzesten Stunden in der Goslarer Geschichte: Im Riechenberger Vertrag verlor die Stadt die Berghoheit, den Zehnten, das Verkaufsrecht für Hüttenerzeugnisse und zwei Drittel der Stadtforst an Braunschweig.

Mühlen- und Brauereiwesen, Schiefer- und Vitriolgewinnung halfen der Stadt zu überleben. Aber im 30jährigen Krieg mußten die Bürger von 1632–1635 die schwedische Besatzung ernähren; die Stadtbrände von 1728 und 1780 vernichteten ganze Quartiere. Ab 1802 geriet Goslar unter ständig wechselnde politische Herrschaft, vermochte sich jedoch dank offensichtlich ausgeprägter Wendehals-Eigenschaften Preußen, Franzosen und Hannoveranern gleich gut anzupassen. Und 1859 war ihr das

the imperial eagle in its coat of arms, Goslar became a free city of the Empire in 1340, a status and title kept until 1802.

The city suffered a serious economic setback when the mines began to flood after 1360. Not until new ideas to drain the mines had been put into practice by 1460 did wealth and power return. Yet it was this show of wealth and power that lead to Goslar's downfall. Having repaid the debt for which the city had held the mines as a security, the envious Dukes of Braunschweig reasserted their control of the mountain. After a bitter feud, the Riechenberg Treaty of 1552 lost the city not only all its rights over the mountain, but also the rights to the tithe, to the sale of the products of its smelters, and on top of it two thirds of the city's forests.

From this blow the city never recovered. Mills and breweries, slate and vitriol production helped it to survive. But during the Thirty Year War the citizens had to feed a Swedish garrison from 1632–1635. And the great fires of 1728 and 1780 destroyed large quarters of the town. From

Der Thronsessel der Salier und Hohenstaufer ist mit seinen romanischen Bronzelehnen (zwischen 1060 und 1080) eine Kostbarkeit. Dieser „Kaiserstuhl" diente bei der Eröffnung des ersten Reichstages im Schloß Charlottenburg 1871 Wilhelm I. und damit letztmalig einem Kaiser als Thron.

The throne of the Salian and Hohenstaufer emperors with its Romanesque armrests (made between 1060 and 1080) is a real treasure. This "Emperor's Chair" saw its last service when Emperor Wilhelm I. sat on it during the opening of the Reichstag (parliament) at Charlottenburg Castle in 1871.

Vor der Pfalz stehen seit der Jahrhundertwende die Reiterstandbilder der beiden Kaiser Wilhelm I. (links) und Friedrich Barbarossa. Auch sie gehörten zum Ziel, im „Nationaldenkmal Pfalz" eine Brücke zwischen dem neuen und dem mittelalterlichen Kaisertum zu schaffen.

Since the turn of the century, the two equestrian statues of Emperors Wilhelm I. and Friedrich Barbarossa mark the approach to the Imperial Palace. They were part of an effort to establish a link between the medieval and the new emperors at this "national monument".

Wirtschaftsglück mit der Entdeckung eines neuen Erzlagers im Rammelsberg wieder hold. Gleichzeitig kehrten Könige und Fürsten wieder in Goslar ein, wenn auch nicht in der Pfalz, so doch in der Kräuterheilanstalt des „Kräuterdoktors" Lampe.

Mit dem Eisenbahnanschluß (1865) fand Goslar den Weg in die Neuzeit mit Industrieansiedlung und der Wohnbebauung über die Wallanlagen hinaus. 1922 wurde es für 50 Jahre kreisfreie Stadt, avancierte im „Dritten Reich" zur „Reichsbauernstadt" und hatte das Glück, den Zweiten Weltkrieg unzerstört zu überstehen. Flüchtlinge und Vertriebene verdoppelten die Einwohnerzahl auf 54 000. Die Folge waren neue Stadtteile im Norden, im Westen dagegen entstand ein ansehnliches Industriegebiet. Die Gebietsreform bescherte 1972 der alten Kaiserstadt vier Töchter: Den Kurort Hahnenklee-Bockswiese, die Dörfer Jerstedt und Hahndorf und die Hüttenstadt Oker.
Mit dem Fall der Zonengrenze haben die Betriebe alte Absatzmärkte zurückgewonnen, und die Stadt ist wieder ein Meilenstein der romanischen Straße des Harzes.

1802 on Goslar had to serve ever changing overlords, but by guile and good luck the city adjusted well in turn to Prussians, French, and Hanoverians. When a new vein was discoverd at the Rammelsberg in 1859, the economy picked up again.

The start into a new era was complete with the railway link in 1865. Factories and living quarters expanded beyond the city walls. From 1922 on Goslar for fifty years regained some administrative independence by becoming a "district-free" town. During the days of the Third Reich it also became "Reichsbauernstadt" (The Reich's Farmer Town) and was lucky enough to escape the terrors of World War II practically unscathed.

The arrival of refugees and deportees from the east doubled the number of inhabitants to 54.000. As a result, new suburbs were developed in the north while a new industrial area grew in the west. With the administrative reforms of 1972, the spa of Hahnenklee-Bockswiese, the villages of Hahndorf and Jerstedt, and the industrial town of Oker with its smelters and heavy industry.

17

Mit dem Mittelalter auf du und du

Die Kaiser sind gegangen, die steinerne Historie ist in Goslar geblieben. Noch immer zeugt das zwischen Breitem Tor und Frankenberger Kirche aufgehängte Oval des Stadtgrundrisses von einem genialen Städteplaner. War es Kaiser Heinrich III. (1039–1056), dessen Herz in der Ulrichskapelle der Kaiserpfalz ruht?

Über diesem Grundriß liegt, die Idee des Gottesstaates verkörpernd, ein von den Altstadtkirchen gebildetes Christuskreuz mit der Marktkirche als Mittelpunkt. Bedeutende Kirchen und Klöster, die wie ein Kranz die Stadt umgaben, brannten die Goslarer 1527 kurzerhand nieder, als der Braunschweiger Erbfeind Herzog Heinrich der Jüngere vor den Toren stand.

Abgebrochen wurde 1820 auch der 1056 von Papst Viktor II. geweihte „Dom", weil das Geld nicht mehr zu seiner Sanierung reichte. Jetzt künden nur noch die eindrucksvolle Vorhalle und der auf dem Parkplatz gepflasterte Grundriß von diesem romanischen Bau, dessen Einfluß

18

Face to Face with the Middle Ages

While the emperors have long gone, their traces in history made of stone have remained in Goslar. Between Breites Tor (Broad Gate) and Frankenberger Kirche (Frankenberg Church), the oval of the original layout of the town still reminds us of the genius who designed it. Was it Emperor Heinrich III. (1039–1056) whose heart rests at the St. Ulrich Chapel of the palace? We do not know.

Yet the layout breathes the air of medieval beliefs. For the Old Town churches form a cross with the Market Church at its center, a symbol of the "City of God". They are all that remains, for the many important churches and monasteries that once surrounded Goslar like a rosary were burned by the citizens in 1527 when their arch-enemy, Duke Heinrich der Jüngere (Henry the Younger) of Braunschweig was before their gates.

Also gone is the "Cathedral". Consecrated in 1056 by Pope Victor II, it was demolished in 1820 because there were no funds for restoring it. Only the

Das Vorbild der Pfalzkapelle St. Ulrich, deren Datierung zwischen 1050 und 1220 schwankt, war das Aachener Münster.

The Palace Chapel of St. Ulrich, dated between 1050 and 1220, was modelled after the minster at Aachen.

Blick vom Turm der Marktkirche auf Kaiserpfalz und Herzberg. Hier standen früher die Turmwächter.

The view from the tower of the Market Church over the Imperial Palace and the Herzberg, was once enjoyed by the guards on the tower.

weit über Goslar hinausging. Mit dem Kaiserstuhl (12. Jh.) bewahrt die Domvorhalle einen kostbaren Schatz.

Die vom Volksmund als Dom eingestufte Stiftskirche war der geistliche Gegenpol zur **Kaiserpfalz**, der berühmtesten kaiserlichen Residenz des 11. bis 13. Jahrhunderts, Lieblingspfalz der Salier, Mittelpunkt des Reiches, an dem die Weichen für europäische Geschichte gestellt wurden. Über hundert Reichs- und Fürstentage fanden in dem um 1050 in seiner prägenden Gestalt errichteten Bau statt. Der fast 50 m lange Reichssaal ist der größte erhaltene Saal einer Pfalz. Auf seine Wände malte zu Ende des vorigen Jahrhunderts Hermann Wislicenus ein historisches Bilderbuch, das mittelalterliche Kaiserherrlichkeit nach 1871 politisch aktualisierte, denn unter Kaiser Wilhelm I. erhielt die Kaiserpfalz die Weihen eines Nationaldenkmals. Kontrapunkt zu den Wandbildern und den Bronzestandbildern Barbarossas und Kaiser Wilhelms I. (um 1900) ist der **„Goslarer Krieger"** im Pfalzgarten, eine Plastik des ersten Goslarer Kaiserringträgers Henry Moore: Der gestürzte Krieger, dem

porch and the outline of the walls in the pavement of the parking lot behind it still tell of the grandeur of this Romanesque building once influential far past the city's borders. With the 12th century throne, the porch holds a great treasure.

Called "cathedral" by the people, the building really was a convent church and as such the spiritual balance to the worldly powers of the imperial palace opposite it. Being the favourite of the Salian emperors, this palace was the navel of the Empire from the 11th to the 13th century, at which European history was made. Built around 1050, the imposing palace saw more than one hundred imperial diets and meetings of nobles. More than 50 metres long, the main Imperial Hall is the largest surviving one. Towards the end of the last century, Hermann Wislicenus painted its walls with historical murals, illustrating the grandeur of medieval emperors with a touch of more recent politics. For with Emperor Wilhelm I. (proclaimed at Versailles 1871) the palace became a sort of national monument.

Die kleinen blühenden Oasen wie der Münzgarten setzen Farbtupfer ins Häusermeer. Oftmals werden sie von reizvollen Skulpturen heimischer Künstler geschmückt.

The Münzgarten is one of many spots of green in a sea of houses. Such flowering oases are often further enhanced by sculptures of local artists.

Im Pfalzgarten ein Anziehungspunkt für Kunstkenner: Henry Moores „Goslarer Krieger" (1975).

Henry Moore's "Goslar Warrior" (1975) at the Palace Gardens is a must for the connoisseur of arts.

der Schild davonrollt, steht wie ein Symbol für den wehrlosen Menschen.

Was die moderne Kunst anbelangt, so zeigt Goslar Flagge. Die Stadt verleiht nicht nur seit 1975 jährlich den Kaiserring, einen weltweit bekannten Kunstpreis, an die bedeutendsten Künstler dieses Jahrhunderts, sondern sie schreibt die Kunst im Stadtbild fort und stellt Einheimi-

A stark contrast to these paintings and the bronze equestrian statues of Emperors Friedrich Barbarossa and Wilhelm I. (about 1900) is the sculpture of the "Goslar Warrior" in the Palace Garden. It was created by Henry Moore, the first recipient of Goslar's modern art award "Kaiserring" and shows a fallen warrior whose shield is rolling away; a symbol of man bereft of defenses.

schen wie Touristen die „Steine des Anstoßes" mitten in den Weg. Den Nagelkopf Reiner Kriesters am Rathaus, die Stahlplatte Richard Serras am Breiten Tor.

Der Hohe Weg mit seiner Königsbrücke, über den einst die Herrscher mit ihrem Gefolge zur Pfalz zogen, verbindet zwei Welten, die kaiserliche und die bürgerliche, die ihr Zentrum auf dem Marktplatz hat. Auf diesem Weg steht das **Große Heilige Kreuz (1254)**: Als Hospital für Pilger, Alte und Kranke wurde es gegründet und hat seine Nutzung bis heute in den Altenwohnungen im Flügelanbau behalten. Die dämmrige Diele mit dem riesigen Kruzifix und den kleinen Kammern der Kunsthandwerker versetzt um Jahrhunderte zurück.

Strahlenförmig läuft auf dem **Marktplatz** das Pflaster auf den Brunnen mit seinen mächtigen romanischen Schalen und dem Goldadler zu. „Der Marktplatz sicher an Architektur einer der schönsten, die es auf der Welt gibt", notierte der Dichter Oskar Loerke im Jahr 1908. Zwei Gebäude, die beide mit ihren Arkaden den Platz weiten, wetteifern miteinander

As for modern art, Goslar certainly makes it stand. Not only does the city award its famous "Kaiserring" year after year since 1975, honouring some of the most important artists of this century. It also introduces modern art to the city, confronting citizens and tourists alike with such controversial pieces as Reiner Kriester's "Nagelkopf" (Head with Nails) at the townhall or Richard Serra's Wall of Steel at the Breites Tor.

The Hohe Weg (Highway) with the Königsbrücke (King's Bridge) once used by the emperors and their retinue on their way to the palace is the link between two worlds, the imperial one and the common one, which had its centre at the market place. Half along this way there stands the Großes Heiliges Kreuz (Great Holy Cross). Founded in 1254 as a hospice for passing pilgrims and the old and sick of the town, it has retained its function until today. A newly restored wing provides housing for the old. Entering it, the dark entrance hall with its large crucifix and the small chambers rented out to artisans move the visitor back in time.

Mitten hinein ins Mittelalter stellen die Stadtväter moderne Kunst: Rainer Kriesters „Nagelkopf" am Rathaus.

As decreed by the city fathers, the Middle Ages meet modern art: Rainer Kriester's "Nagelkopf" (Head with Nails) at the townhall.

Ein großartiges Ensemble: Markkirche, Rathaus und Marktbrunnen.

A magnificent ensemble: the Market Church, the townhall, and the market fountain.

24

um den ersten Rang. **Rathaus (Kernbau um 1450)** und „Kaiserworth", das 500 Jahre alte Gildehaus der reichen Fernhandelskaufleute. Seit man bei der Sanierung der Fassade ihre ursprüngliche, aufgemalte Renaissance-Diamantquaderung entdeckte und rekonstruierte, scheint es dem Rathaus die Schau zu stehlen. Aber eben nur „scheint". Die imposante Diele des Rathauses mit ihrer sternenübersäten blauen Holzdecke und ihren Geweihleuchtern verrät viel über das Selbstbewußtsein der Bürger, denen der Rammelsberg in jenen Jahrzehnten die Kassen füllte. Aber dann ist es der rundum mit Sibyllen, Kaisern und biblischen Darstellungen ausgemalte **„Huldigungssaal" (1500)**, der den Besucher in seinen Bann schlägt. Dieses Sitzungszimmer des

Like rays from the sun the pavement radiates from the fountain at the center of the marketplace. With its impressive Romanesque basins and the golden eagle on top, the fountain underlines the words of the poet Oskar Loerke, who claimed in 1908 that "this marketplace is certainly among the most splendid architectural achievements found on earth." Two buildings, both with arcades, vie with each other for first place: the townhall (core built about 1450) and the "Kaiserworth", the 500 years old guildhall of the wealthy merchants. Since the original design of the Renaissance diamond ornamentation was discovered and restored during the recent renovation of the facade, the "Kaiserworth" seems to succeed in this contest. But it only seems. For it cannot

Marktbrunnen: Der Goslarer Adler gleicht einem Märchenvogel (links), aber im Brunnenbecken herrscht Kampf: Der Drache verschlingt einen Menschen. Blick vom Marktplatz zum Schuhhof (rechts.)

The Market fountain: The Goslar Eagle rivals the birds of fairy tales (left), but down in the basin the fight is on as a dragon devours a human. A view from the market-place to the Schuhof (right).

Das Glockenspiel zeigt den Erzabbau im Mittelalter.

The figures at the chimes show the mining of ore in the Middle Ages.

Rates mit seiner Trinitatiskapelle gehört zu den Stars spätgotischer Innenausstattungen im weltlichen Bereich.

Vom Rathaus spannt sich der Bogen zum Bergwerk, der Quelle kaiserlichen und bürgerlichen Reichtums. Über tausend Jahre wurden hier zunächst Gold, Silber, später Zink und Blei abgebaut. Ein Blick aus der Rathausdiele hinüber zum Kämmereiamt rückt das Bergwerk wie im Vergrößerungsglas heran. Um 9, 12, 15 und 18 Uhr erscheinen Ritter Ramm und sein Pferd, das der Sage nach die erste Silberader am Rammelsberg freischarrte, nebst Kaiser Otto I. Bergleute aus verschiedenen Jahrhunderten verraten ihre Abbaumethoden. Wenn das "Glückauf, der Steiger kommt" ertönt, hat der **Brunnenadler** Mühe, seinen Platz unter den Touristen zu behaupten. Zumal er nur eine Kopie ist, deren Original im Rathaus steht, weil immer wieder böse Buben ihm die Flügel rupften oder die Beine brachen. Eine goldene Konkurrenz präsentiert das an der "Kaiserworth" hockende **Dukatenmännchen**, nur klemmt sein Golddukaten schon seit Jahrhunderten fest.

really compete with the breathtaking sights the townhall has to offer. Its hall with its blue, star-spangled ceiling and its chandeliers made from antlers tell a lot of the self-confidence of a people whose chests in those days were filled by the Rammelsberg mines. Even more imposing is the Huldigungssaal (Hall of Homage) of about 1500 with its paintings of sibyls, emperors, and biblical motives. This committee room of the town councillors, and the adjoining Trinitatiskapelle (Trinity Chapel) are among the "stars" of profane Late Gothic interior.

In Goslar the mines are never far. The sparkling treasure of the Huldigungssaal is the Bergkanne of 1477, a large silver vessel named so for its ornaments from life in the mines. As if through a magnifying glass, a look out of the windows of the hall to the city treasury across the market place brings the mines into view. Every three hours from 9 a.m. to 6 p.m. the chimes play their songs and figures move along, among them the knight Ramm, whose pawing horse according to legend laid bare the first gold vein, Emperor Otto I, and miners from different centuries showing their tools of trade.

Die sogenannte Schwurhand aus der Trinitatiskapelle im Rathaus, die ein Armreliquiar von 1300 ist, weist auf den Huldigungssaal (Seite 30/31) hin.

The so-called "Hand of Oath" from the Trinity Chapel at the townhall, a 13th century armreliquary, points to the Huldigungssaal (Hall of Homage), pp. 30/31.

Hinter Wandgemälden verborgen: Die Trinitatiskapelle im Huldigungssaal mit Schmerzensmann und Schmerzensmutter auf den Innentüren und Darstellung der Leidensgeschichte Jesu an den Wänden.

Hidden behind murals: the Trinitatiskapelle in the Huldigungssaal with paintings of a man and a mother of pain on the doors' insides and the ordeals of Jesus on the walls.

Zur Tausendjahr-Feier im Jahr 1922 stiftete der Hannoversche Städtetag der Stadt Goslar acht Glasscheiben für die Maßwerkfenster der Däle. Sie wurden von dem Kölner Glasmaler Hans Zepter geschaffen und 1929 eingebaut. In den Giebelfenstern befinden sich die Wappen der Stifterstädte, unter ihnen an der Marktfront Szenen aus der Geschichte Goslars.

For the millenary celebrations in 1922, the Hannoversche Städtetag donated eight stained glass windows for the windows of the hall. Created by the Cologne artist Hans Zepter they were eventually put in place in 1929. In the gable windows the coats of arms of the donating communities are displayed while below scenes from Goslar's past are shown.

Das Rathaus und die Ratskirche (Marktkirche St. Cosmas und Damian) bilden ein eindrucksvoll gestaffeltes Ensemble.

The town hall and the market church of St Cosmas and Damian form an impressive ensemble.

In ihrem wiederentdeckten ockerroten Renaissance-Gewand mit Diamantquader ist die "Kaiserworth" der Blickfang des Marktplatzes. Mit ihr demonstrierten die Fernhandelskaufleute ihren Reichtum. Die kaiserlichen Majestäten bezogen ihren Platz an der Fassade erst später, aber noch rechtzeitig genug, um Heine 1824 zu der spöttischen Bemerkung zu veranlassen, sie sähen aus wie "gebratene Universitätspedelle." Unter den bizarren Wasserspeiern, Masken und Nakkedeis, die die Fassade bevölkern, ist das Dukatenmännchen der unbestrittene Star. Die stattliche "Kaiserworth" wie das Rathaus öffnen sich mit ihren Arkaden dem Marktplatz und vermitteln Weite.

Dressed again in its original Renaissance colours, the ochre-red facade of the "Kaiserworth" with its diamond-square ornaments has become a focal point of the market place. This way the merchant guild once demonstrated its wealth. The statues of the emperors were added later, but still early enough to allow Heine his sarcastic comment that "they looked like fried university janitors". Among the multitude of bizarre gargoyles, masks and naked characters, the "Dukatenmännchen" has remained the unrivalled star. The arcades of the town hall as well as those of the magnificent Kaiserworth open on the market place to create a feeling of wide and open space.

Das Straßencafe der "Kaiserworth" bietet Logenplätze für das Glockenspiel (oben links). Leider hat das Dukatenmännchen seit Jahrhunderten die "Dukaten-Produktion" eingestellt. Kaiserliche Majestäten bewachen die Hotelgäste im Obergeschoß des Hauses. (oben rechts).

The street café of the "Kaiserworth" offers the box seats for a view of the chimes (top left). Too bad, the Dukatenmännchen has quit producing ducats centuries ago. Imperial majesties guard the hotel guests in the upper rooms of the house (top right).

Das Brusttuch, das sein Baumeister auf ein dreieckiges Grundstück zauberte, ist eines der schönsten Goslarer Patrizierhäuser. Wie ein Lesebuch für Gelehrte nimmt sich sein Schnitzwerk aus, sehr stattlich auch das Bäckergildehaus (1501) in unmittelbarer Nachbarschaft.

The Brusttuch, miraculously placed on a triangular plot by its master builder, is one of Goslar's finest patrician houses. Its inscriptions are a reader for the scholar. The nearby Bakers' guildhall of 1501 is another of those magnificent buildings.

Wo sich heute die stattlichen Bürgerhäuschen am Schuhhof präsentieren, standen einst die alten Marktbuden, die über keinen Hofraum verfügten.

Today's stately houses at the Schuhhof have taken the place of the tiny market stalls of old that didn't even have a yard.

Konkurrenz bekommt der Marktplatz im benachbarten **Schuhhof**, der ältesten Platzanlage. Ihn säumen die Arkaden des Schuhmacher-Gildehauses, die Hirsch-Apotheke und stattliche Häuser, deren Fachwerk wie Hexenstich wirkt. Sie sind aus den ehemaligen Marktbuden hervorgegangen. Noch steht eine uralte Linde als Rechtsdenkmal in der Mitte des Platzes. 400 Jahre mag sie alt sein.

Nebenan beginnt die Münzstraße mit Hausgestalten, die sich im Obergeschoß trotz ihres hohen Alters offensichtlich zu küssen begehren. In ihrem Schutz gelangt man – wie in einer Zeitmaschine ins Mittelalter – zum **„Weißen Schwan"**, einem alten Ausspann. Blumen umranken die 350 Jahre alten Gebäude mit ihren Schnitzereien wie auf einer Insel der Romantik.

Dazu gibt es Goslar-Geschichte in Zinn. Das **Zinnfigurenmuseum** führt mit seinen Guckkästen auf die reizvollste Art an die Brennpunkte der regionalen Geschichte. Zeuge der Finanzgeschichte ist die „Münze", der stattliche Rest des städtischen Münzhofes (1500).

A serious competitor to the marketplace is the neighbouring Schuhhof, the oldest plaza in town lined by the arcades of the former cobblers' guildhall, the Hirschapotheke (Stag Pharmacy), and magnificent houses with exquisitely patterned timber framework, which developed from earlier market stalls. An ancient linden tree of some 400 years still stands in the center of the plaza, a symbol of the justice of old.

Next to it one enters the Münzstraße where figures in the upper storeys inspite of their age still seem to desire to kiss each other. As if stepping aboard a time machine to the Middle Ages under their caring glances, one moves on to the "Weißer Schwan" (White Swan), once a horse station for passing coaches. Flowers twine around the 350 years old buildings with their carved beams, creating a romantic island. An added flavour is the Museum of Pewter Figures where carefully designed dioramas bring to life some key events in regional history. A witness to Goslar's historic role in the world of money are the impressive remains of the municipal mint, built around 1500.

Die Münzstraße, überragt von den Türmen der Marktkirche, ist eine stille Straße mit dem Münzgarten am Weg, dem „Weißen Schwan", dem Zinnfigurenmuseum und der alten Münze.

With the towers of the Market Church behind it, the Münzstraße is a rather quiet street along with the Münzgarten, the "White Swan", the pewter museum, and the old mint.

Deutlich läßt sich im „Weißen Schwan" an der Gruppierung der Gebäude um den Hof die Situation des historischen Ausspanns ablesen.

At the White Swan, the arrangements of the buildings around the yard tells of the practical needs of the historic horse changing station.

Auch wenn ein böswilliger Reiseschriftsteller 1793 notierte, geistreiche Physiognomien seien in Goslar nicht zu entdecken, war zumindest der Magister Thiling, der 1521 das **Brusttuch am Hohen Weg** erbaute, ein gelehrter Berg- und Hüttenherr. Er ließ den Braunschweiger Bildschnitzer Stappen an dem heutigen Hotel den römisch-griechischen Götterhimmel in Holz bannen. Moderne Zeitgenossen, wenn vielleicht auch geistreicher (ausschauend) als vor 200 Jahren, haben es schwer, die bedeutungsschweren Symbole zu entschlüsseln. Zwischen die antiken Schönheiten schmuggelte Stappen Dukatenmännchen und Butterhanne. Über letztere notierte 1875 ein spitzzüngiger Besucher im Gästebuch des "Brusttuchs": "Mit der linken Hand da buttert sie, die rechte am Gesäße, / so macht man hierzuland den guten Harzer Käse".

Die Butterhanne am Brusttuch und das Dukatenmännchen an der "Kaiserworth" sind (heftige) Konkurrenten um die Gunst des Publikums. Gemeinsam ist ihnen die freigelegte "Sitzfläche". Das Aussprechen der genauen volkstümlichen Bezeichnung für

Even though an ill-meaning author of travel books noted in 1793 that intelligent faces were not to be found in Goslar, at least Magister Thiling, who built the **Brusttuch at the Hoher Weg** in 1521, must have been a very educated man; for he commissioned the master wood-carver Stappen from Braunschweig to once more immortalise the Roman and Greek gods and goddesses in the wooden ornaments of today's hotel building. And while modern men may look more intelligent than their forebears 200 years ago, they have more difficulties to understand the old symbols. Among the ancient gods, the Dukatenmännchen and the Butterhanne come as a surprise. As to the latter, in 1875 a witty guest noted in the hotel's guest-book: "Churning the butter with the left, holding the right to the behind, / the locals make the Harz cheese, the tastiest of its kind.

The Butterhanne at the "Brusttuch" and the Dukatenmännchen at the "Kaiserworth" are for ever vying for the favourable attention of the visitors. Their common denominator is the bare behind. Daring to name this part of the

Die Blumen an der Abzucht werden durch eine Zeitungsinitiative finanziert, unter anderem über Bußgelder für nicht salonfähige Wörter.

The flowers at the Abzucht are an initiative of the local newspaper and financed, among other things, by fines levied for the use of objectionable words.

die verlängerte Wirbelsäule wird in Goslar mit einer Mark Bußgeld geahndet, denn mit diesen Bußgeldern finanziert die Goslarsche Zeitung die Bepflanzung der Blumenkästen am Goslarer Hausflüßchen, der Abzucht. Es gab bereits recht prominente Sünder, die dank ihrer Strafgelder Petunien und Geranien zu schönster Blüte verhalfen: Bundeskanzler Helmut Schmidt, Außenminister Hans-Dietrich Genscher und Porzellankönig Philip Rosenthal. Vor allem aber gibt es Bürger, die die Pflege der Blumenkästen übernehmen.

Die Abzucht, die bei Hochwasser wie ein kleiner Mississippi einherbraust, schlängelt sich üblicherweise gemächlich an den alten Häusern vorbei und begrüßt die unterschiedlichsten Anlieger: Gefängnis, Hospital, Kneipe, Museum und Kapelle. Sie war einst die schmutzige Tochter der Gose, die mit dem zunehmenden Erzabbau die schadstoffbefrachteten Abwässer des Berges übernahm, während die Gose als Trinkwasserkanal geführt wurde. Heute sind wieder Forellen ihre Bewohner.

prolonged spine by its vulgar name demands a fine of 1,– DM, the proceeds of which are used by the local newspaper "Goslarsche Zeitung" to finance the planting of flowers along Goslar's "house-river", the Abzucht. Among the more prominent sinners whose fines helped geraniums and petunias to flower were the former Chancellor Helmut Schmidt, the former Minister of Foreign Affairs Hans-Dietrich Genscher, and industrialist Philip Rosenthal (manufacturer of precious china). But all their contributions would be in vain if it weren't for the citizens who care for the plants day by day.

The Abzucht, which at times of high water may thunder along like a Mississippi River in miniature, usually babbles away peacefully, passing the most diverse neighbours from jail to hospice and on to inn, museum, and finally chapel. Running with all the heavily polluted waste water from the mines, it used to be the "dirty daughter" of the Gose, which had been turned into a drinking water channel running under the city. Today trouts have returned.

Am romantischen „Wasserloch" schlängelt sich die Abzucht durch den Mauerring und verläßt die Innenstadt.

Winding its way through the townwall, the Abzucht leaves the inner city at the romantic "Water Hole".

Die original erhaltene Lohmühle (1532) gehört zu den Attraktionen an der Abzucht. Um 1200 existierten 27 Wassermühlen in Goslar.

The Lohmühle (Tanners' Mill) of 1532 withstood the passing times and is now one of the attractions at the Abzucht. Around 1200 there were 27 water mills in Goslar.

Links: Die alte Stadt schmückt sich von Frühjahr bis Herbst mit leuchtenden Farben. Blumen geben den Brückchen über die Abzucht und der kühlen Front des Großen Heiligen Kreuzes Charme

Left: From spring to autumn the old town dresses in shining colours. Flowers add charm to the bridges over the Abzucht and the cool facade of the Großes Heiliges Kreuz.

Rechts: Maler Herbst setzt verschwenderisch rote, grüne und gelbe Farbtupfer rund um die Türme der Marktkirche

Right: Autumn, the great painter of nature, squanders its wealth of colours around the towers of the market church.

Kein Weg führt an **St. Stephani** vorbei, das wie eine Glucke die Unterstadt behütet. 1728 war die nach dem Vorbild des Domes erbaute romanische Kirche ein Raub der Flammen geworden, aber bereits sechs Jahre später konnte der neue Barockbau geweiht werden. Sie markiert die Haupteinfallsstraße der aus Richtung Osten kommenden Touristen, die Breite Straße, deren Breite aber nur sogenannt ist. Deswegen sind die Stadtväter bemüht, die motorisierten Besucher mit Hilfe eines ausgeklügelten Verkehrsleitsystems um die Stadt herum auf die großen Parkplätze zu locken.

Wie aus dem Märchen entstiegen, liegt das **St. Annenhaus** an der Abzucht. Es ist eines der drei Goslarer Hospitäler, 1488 von der Familie Bornhusen gestiftet. Das enge Miteinander von geistlichem und weltlichem Bereich, von Kapelle und Wohnraum, macht seine einmalige Atmosphäre aus. Kein Wunder, daß das St. Annenhaus gern für Konzerte und Lesungen genutzt wird. Neben romanischen und gotischen Kruzifixen und Heiligenfiguren verfügt die Kapelle mit dem Margarethenteppich über ein

The Church of St. Stephani, watching over the Lower Town like a mother hen over her chicks, can't be missed. The original building, modelled after the cathedral, fell victim to the great fire of 1728, but only six years later the new Baroque building was consecrated. It marks the main access route for tourists approaching from the east, coming up the Breite Straße (Broadway), the name of which is a misnomer for today's traffic needs. Because of this, the city fathers try their best to lure the motorized tourists to the large parking lots on the periphery of the old city core by means of a rather ingenious traffic guiding system and maze of one-way streets.

As if sprung from a fairytale, the St. Annenhaus lies at the banks of the Abzucht. It is one of the three hospices of medieval Goslar, established by the Bornhusen family in 1488. With chapel and living quarters being virtually one, this close intertwining of the spiritual and the profane make for a very special atmosphere. Small wonder that the St. Annenhaus is much favoured for concerts and readings. In addition to Roman-

Blick durch das große Tor auf das St. Annenhaus.

Looking through the big gate at the St. Annenhaus (St. Ann's House).

In der Däle des spätgotischen Hospitals St. Annen befindet sich eine reich ausgestattete Kapelle mit bedeutenden Kruzifixen und dem St. Margarethenteppich (14. Jh.).

The entrance hall of the Late Gothic hospice of St. Annen is the home of a richly furnished chapel holding important crucifixes and the 14th century St. Margaret's tapestry

Blütenzauber an der St. Stephanikirche. Die ursprünglich romanische Kirche wurde ein Opfer der Feuersbrunst von 1728. Der Neubau, eine barocke dreischiffige Hallenkirche, konnte schon 1734 geweiht werden.

The romance of blossoming trees at the Church of St. Stephen. The original Romanesque church fell victim to the great fire of 1728. The new building, a three-naved Baroque hall church, was consecrated in 1734.

Das Amtshaus der Tuchmacher und Walker nennt man wegen der runenartigen Meisterzeichen auf der Schwelle des Obergeschosses „Runenhaus".

The guildhall of the clothmakers and fullers is called "the house of runes" because of the rune-like master and guild marks carved into the beams of the upper floor.

besonderes Prunkstück. In 32 gestickten Bildfeldern werden Leben und Martyrium der heiligen Margarethe erzählt.

Bei St. Annen steht man am Kreuzweg. Folgt man der Abzucht, führt sie den Besucher zum stattlichen **„Runenhaus"**, 1551 erbaut als Amtshaus der Tuchmacher und Walker, und weiteren wunderhübschen Fachwerkhäuschen.

Die Alternative bietet die Glockengießerstraße, die ein Weg in Goslars wehrhafte Vergangenheit ist. Die alte **Stadtmauer** mißt an dieser Stelle stolze sieben Meter und wird bewacht von dem halbrunden Kegelwortturm. An der Mauerstraße stehen noch dessen heute friedlich bewohnte „Kollegen", der Teufelsturm und der Weberturm, bei dem sogar noch der Wehrgang erhalten ist. Von der Existenz der anderen Türme berichten nur Reste. Die Abzucht hat ihre eigene Toranlage im Mauerring und schlüpft durch das „Wasserloch" aus der Altstadt. In ihrer Nähe befindet sich der jüdische Friedhof, der die Gewaltherrschaft des „Dritten Reiches" unzerstört überstanden hat.

Paradestücke des Goslarer Verteidigungswillen sind der

esque and Gothic crucifixes and statues of saints, the chapel treasures the Margarethenteppich (St. Margareta Tapestry). 32 distinct embroideries tell of the saint's life and martyrdom.

At St. Annen one stands at a crossroads. Following the waters of the Abzucht, one reaches the impressive Runenhaus (House of Runes) of 1551, once the residence of the clothmakers and fullers guild, and further beautiful half-timbered houses.

The alternative route follows the Glockengießerstraße (Bell-Founders-Street) and provides some insight into Goslar's medieval defences. Here the old townwall is seven metres wide at the base and is guarded by the semi-circular Kegelwortturm. Two of its counterparts are found on the Mauerstraße (Wallstreet), the Teufelsturm (Devil's Tower) and the Weberturm (Weavers' Tower) with its parapet walk still intact. Both are still lived in today. Of the other flanking towers only vague traces are left. The waters of the Abzucht have their own fortified gate when they finally leave the Old Town at the Wasserloch (Water Hole). Nearby is the

Am Brunnen vor dem Tore: Er befindet sich am Breiten Tor und ist das Ende einer "Wasserreise", einer hölzernen Wasserleitung.

"The well before the gates" lies at the Breite Tor and is the end of a wooden water duct.

Der Werderhof, einst Torkaserne der Söldner am Breiten Tor, ist heute Gästehaus eines Goslarer Unternehmes

Once the barracks of the soldiers at the Breites Tor, the Werderhof is now used as a guest-house by a Goslar business.

wuchtige **Zwinger** mit seinen sechs Meter dicken Mauern auf dem Thomaswall und das Breite Tor – damals eine der mächtigsten Toranlagen im Reich. Im Jahr 1517 wurde der Zwinger errichtet und trug bis 1857 noch ein spitzes Kegeldach als Hütchen. Eine Rüstkammer im obersten Geschoß illustriert den Erfindungsreichtum unserer Altvorderen auf dem Sektor der Waffen und nicht zuletzt der Folterinstrumente. Eingerahmt ist der Turm von den früher zu den Befestigungsanlagen gehörendem Kahnteich und dem Judenteich.

Rasselnd ließen die Goslarer am **Breiten Tor** die Fallgitter nieder, wenn die Braunschweiger Feinde ante portas standen. Der mit einer Kaiserfigur sozusagen als Drohgebärde geschmückte Flankierungsturm, der Rißlingsturm, ist 42 m hoch. In der ehemaligen Söldnerkaserne, dem Werderhof, befindet sich heute das Gästehaus eines Goslarer Unternehmens. Durch das schmiedeeiserne Tor eines Turmes der Toranlage fällt der Blick auf die Gedenkstätte Brieg, war doch Goslar die erste westdeutsche Stadt, die nach 1945 eine Patenschaft für eine schlesische

old Jewish cemetery which escaped damage during the Third Reich.

The most impressive demonstrations of Goslar's will to self-defence are the collossal Zwinger at the Thomaswall, a magnificent tower with walls six metres thick, and the Breite Tor (Broad Gate) – then one of the strongest fortified gates throughout the empire. The Zwinger was built in 1517, and until 1857 it was crowned by a conical helm roof. An armoury at the top floor illustrates the inventiveness of our ancestors with respect to weapons and even more so to instruments of torture. The ponds on either side, the Kahnteich in front and the two Judenteiche, once were part of the city's fortifications.

Noisily Goslarians closed the portcullis when their enemies from Braunschweig were before the gates once more. To underline the status of imperial free city, the 42 metres high, flanking Rißlingturm even features a statue of the emperor. The former garrison quarters, the so-called Werderhof, now is the guest house of a Goslar business. Looking through the wrought-iron gate

Im Schutz des Breiten Tores werden sich die Goslarer einst sicher gefühlt haben. Während diese mittelalterliche Befestigungsanlage (um 1500) die Zeiten überdauerte, wütete im 18. Jh. in der Breiten Straße der Rote Hahn.
Goslarians once felt safe behind the fortifications of the Breites Tor. While this medieval bulwark of about 1500 survived the times, the houses at the Breite Straße were devoured by flames in the 18th century.

Das Breite Tor mit seinen zyklopischen Türmen; in der Mitte die Stahlplatte des Goslarer Kaiserringträgers Richard Serra.
The Breite Tor with its cycloplike towers; between them the steel plate by Richard Serra, one of holders of Goslar's Kaiserring award.

Stadt übernahm und heute Kontakte mit dem polnischen Brieg unterhält. Insgesamt besaß die Freie Reichsstadt um 1500 50 Befestigungstürme und mindestens ebenso viele Mauerreiter. Für die in friedlicher Absicht erscheinenden Touristen sind sie heute überflüssig geworden.

Am ehemaligen **Rosentor** macht der Achtermann-Flankierungsturm dem Zwinger Konkurrenz. Er ist von einer Hotelanlage „umkleidet", und aus seinem Erdgeschoß ist nach der Verwendung als Schafstall ein Restaurant geworden. Im vorigen Jahrhundert wurden bis auf das Breite Tor die Stadttore weitgehend abgebrochen. Nur die Reste des Rosentores vermitteln noch einen schwachen Abglanz der Stadt, die keineswegs Krethi und Plethi in ihre Mauern einließ.

Um 1800 entmilitarisierte Bürgermeister Johann Georg Siemens die Wallanlagen und schuf anmutige Grüngürtel rund um die Stadt. (Entmilitarisiert wurde übrigens auch gut 150 Jahre später nach dem Zweiten Weltkrieg der Goslarer Flugplatz auf dem Wege friedlicher Demontage, indem man ihn durch Bebau-

of the tower, one has a glimpse of the Brieg memorial, a sign of Goslar's partnership with the formerly Silesian city of Brieg, and proof of the continuing contact with the now Polish town. All told, by 1500 the Free Imperial City of Goslar was fortified by a system of walls with 50 towers and at least as many bartizans not longer in use against the peaceful invasions by the multitudes of tourists.

The flanking tower of the Achtermann at the former Rosentor in some ways is a competitor in size to the Zwinger. Today it has become part of a hotel complex and its groundfloor, in between used as a sheepcote, has been turned into a restaurant. With the exception of the Breite Tor, all gates were torn down during the last century. Still, the remains of the Rosentor afford a glimpse of the wealth of the town that did not suffer just any Tom, Dick and Harry within its walls.

Around 1800 mayor Johann Georg Siemens had the walls demilitarized and turned into a pleasant green belt around the city. (In some ways a precedence to a second time of

Ein wunderhübsches Gartenhäuschen inmitten von Kleingärten.

A beautiful pavilion amidst small garden plots with the Church of St. Stephen in the background.

Wie eine Glucke ragt St. Stephani über der Dächerlandschaft auf, vorn rechts die Stadtmauer mit dem halbrunden Kegelwortturm (1459).

Like a mothering hen the Church of St. Stephen towers above the sea of roofs; to the right the remains of the townwall with the semi-circular flanking Kegelwortturm of 1459.

ung außer Betrieb setzte). Die Siemens sind in Goslar urkundlich seit 1384 nachweisbar und haben im 18. Jahrhundert vier Bürgermeister gestellt. Der reiche Handelsherr **Hans Siemens** errichtete 1693 das Stammhaus in der Schreiberstraße 12, das sich noch heute im Familienbesitz befindet und Standort der jährlichen Familientreffen ist. Es ist Goslars größtes Bürgerhaus aus dem 17. Jahrhundert.

Aus dem Gewirr der roten und blauen Dächer ragen Goslars Kirchen mit ihren gewaltigen Westwerken auf. Den Höhenrekord von 66 m halten die beiden unterschiedlichen Türme der aus dem 12. Jahrhundert stammenden **Marktkirche**. Sie war die alte Ratskirche. Glockengießermeister Magnus Karsten schuf die herrliche Bronzetaufe. Sein prächtiges Haus (1573) steht noch heute an der Bergstraße gegenüber dem Siemenshaus. In besonderer Weise verbinden jedoch die Glasfenster der Marktkirche Romanik und 20. Jahrhundert. Um 1230 wurde der heute in Norddeutschland einzigartige Zyklus mit dem Martyrium der beiden Namenspatrone der Kirche, der Heiligen Cosmas

56

demilitarization when Goslar's airfield was given to a more sensible usage by turning it into a housing development.) The Siemens family, by the way, has resided in Goslar since 1384, and in the 18th century four mayors of this family served the town. In 1693, the wealthy merchant Hans Siemens had his residence built at Schreiberstraße 12. Being the largest of Goslar's 17th century patrician houses, the building has been in the possession of the family ever since and serves as the place of the regular family meetings.

Goslar's churches with their massive westworks tower above the multitude of red and blue roofs. The record is held by the two different towers of the 12th century Market Church, once the church of the town council. Its magnificent bronze baptismal font was created by the master bell-founder Magnus Karsten. His splendid house, built in 1573, is found opposite the Siemenshaus on the Bergstraße. The stained glass windows of the Market Church link the Romanesque past to the 20th century present. Singular to the north of Germany is the cycle depicting

Von dem um die Jahrhundertwende geschaffenen Bismarckdenkmal auf dem Georgenberg hat man einen wundervollen Blick auf Goslar.

From the Bismarck Monument on the Georgenberg, erected around the turn of the century, one has a splendid view over Goslar.

Die Kirchtürme sind unübersehbare Markierungspunkte im Häusergewimmel.

The church towers are the beacons in the sea of houses.

und Damian, geschaffen. Mit den in einer Vitrine untergebrachten Glasbildern korrespondierten die eindrucksvollen abstrakten Chorfenster von Johannes Schreiter (1991), einem der bekanntesten Glasmaler der Gegenwart.

Die 47 Kirchen, Kapellen und Klöster des Mittelalters verschafften Goslar den Beinamen „Nordisches Rom". Alle Altstadtkirchen bis auf St. Stephani, das nach einem Brand 1734 als barocker Phönix aus der romanischen Asche wieder erstand, haben einen romanischen Kern. Stilrein romanisch erhalten ist bis heute das Juwel Neuwerk (1186), dessen strenger Raumeindruck überwältigt. Mit dem reichen Steinmetzschmuck an der Hauptapsis und den Fresken im Chor ist es Goslars eindrucksvollste Kirche. An den übrigen Kirchen bauten über die Jahrhunderte Gotik, Renaissance und Barock mit Seitenschiffen, Kanzeln, Orgelemporen und Altären weiter, ohne den romanischen Grundakkord zum Verstummen zu bringen.

Die katholische **St. Jakobikirche (1073)** hütet die bedeutendste mittelalterliche Gosla-

the martyrdom of the church's patron saints, St. Cosmas and St. Demian. Created around 1230 and kept in a glass showcase, the stained glass paintings correspond well with the abstract stained glass windows of the choir, created in 1991 by Johannes Schreiter, one of the best glass painters of today.

In the Middle Ages, 47 churches, chapels, and monasteries earned the city the title "Rome of the North". With the exception of St. Stephani, which in 1734 emerged again from the ashes of a devastating fire like a Baroque phoenix, all Old Town churches have a Romanesque core. The crown belongs to the former Benedictine abbey Neuwerk, virtually unaltered since it was built in 1186. The relative austerity of its inside is overwhelming, and with the rich masonry of its apse and the frescos of the choir it certainly is Goslar's most impressive church. In all other churches, the building activies of the eras from Gothic to Renaissance and Baroque all have left their traces in aisles, pulpits, organ galleries and altars, but never did they silence the underlying and ever permeating Romanesque accord.

Zwischen Baum und Marienkapelle des Rathauses schiebt sich der Hohe Chor der Marktkirche mit den modernen Fenstern von Johannes Schreiter.

The chevet of the Market Church with its modern windows by Johannes Schreiter shows between the tree and the townhall's St. Mary's Chapel.

Die modernen Chorfenster in der Marktkirche korrespondieren mit dem Barockaltar, vorn die Kanzel (1581).

The modern windows of the choir correspond with the Baroque altar, in the foreground the pulpit of 1581.

„Mann und Frau" nennen die Goslarer die beiden ungleichen Türme der Marktkirche (1151), die als Hauptpfarrkirche größer als die übrigen Goslarer Kirchen ist.

The rather unequal towers of the Market Church (1151) are dubbed "husband and wife" by the locals. Being the main parish church it is larger than the other churches of Goslar.

Die Kirche St. Jakobi (1073) ist bisher die einzige Altstadtkirche, die bei der Restaurierung ihr ursprüngliches Putzkleid zurückerhielt. Deswegen leuchten auch ihre Türme weithin.

St. Jacob's Church (1073) is the only Old Town church which was restored to its original plaster facade. This is why its towers are shining from afar.

rer Skulptur, eine ergreifende Pieta des mitteldeutschen Meisters Hans Witten (1520), die man als „Berg des Leidens" bezeichnet hat. In die Stadtmauer eingebaut ist die **Frankenberger Kirche**, die den höchsten Standort bezogen hat und mit ihrer eleganten barocken Turmhaube über die Stadt schaut. Die strenge romanische Westempore (13. Jh.) ist ein attraktiver Gegensatz zur reichen barocken Ausstattung dieser wohl intimsten Goslarer Kirche. Sie und die Klauskapelle, eine im 12. Jahrhundert errichtete Stadttorkapelle, standen in enger Beziehung zu den Berg-

The Catholic Church of St. Jacob treasures Goslar's most important medieval sculpture, a pieta by the Middle German master Hans Witten (1520), often named "the Mountain of Sorrow". Having been made part of the townwall, the Frankenberg Church with its elegant Baroque steeple takes the geographically highest position overlooking the town. The strictly Romanesque west gallery is a stark but attractive contrast to the otherwise richly Baroque interior of this probably most intimate of Goslar's churches. The Frankenberg Church and the nearby Klaus Chapel, a

Unverzagt reiht sich das Ratsgymnasium von 1888 (links) in die kirchliche Phalanx von Neuwerk (Mitte) und St. Jakobi ein.

Undaunted, the Ratsgymnasium of 1888 (left) joins the phalanx of churches with the Neuwerk Church (centre) the St. Jacob's Church.

Eine Schönheit im Grünen ist die Frankenberger Kirche mit ihrem eleganten Turm.

The Frankenberger Kirche with its elegant steeple is a sleeping beauty amidst green.

leuten. Der Kapelle, in der zu Schichtbeginn Andachten für die Bergleute stattfanden, war ein Bergmannshospital angegliedert. Die Dritte im Bunde ist die kleine Schwester des Großen Heiligen Kreuzes, das **Kleine Heilige Kreuz** am Frankenberger Plan.

Den **Krodoaltar (um 1129)**, der in der Salierausstellung in Speyer als „goldener Altar" Furore machte, und das **Goslarer Evangeliar (um 1230)**, von Fachleuten als künstlerisch wertvoller eingeschätzt als das Evangeliar Heinrichs des Löwen, sollte kein Goslar-Besucher auslassen. In der neu gestalteten Kirchenabteilung des städtischen Museums sind diese Kostbarkeiten umgeben von Ausstattungsstücken des Doms, einer riesigen Kreuzigungsgruppe (1520), die einst den Lettner des Domes akzentuierte, Rücklaken des Chorherrengestühls, dem ältesten Goslarer Glasbild, romantischen Madonnen und gotischen Altären.

Auch vor den Toren der Stadt warten interessante Kirchen auf den Besucher: Die Ruine der **Stiftskirche Riechenberg** mit einer Krypta (1150), an deren Kapitellen lombardi-

12th century gate chapel, were closely linked to the life of the miners. Here services were held at the beginning of a shift. A miners' hospital was also attached to the chapel. The third to complete the ensemble was the Kleines Heiliges Kreuz (Small Holy Cross) at the Frankenberger Plan, the smaller sister to the hospice of the Großes Heiliges Kreuz.

No visitor to Goslar should miss the city's museum, for its newly arranged department of religious arts presents such exhibts as the 1120 Krodo Altar, which was dubbed "Golden Altar" and as such caused a sensation when featured at the special exhibition on the era of the Salian emperors at Speyer. Also shown is the Goslar Evangeliar of 1230, which experts consider artistically more valuable than the Evangeliar of Heinrich der Löwe (Henry the Lion). A huge crucifix of 1520 that once highlighted the choir screen at the cathedral, the back cloth of the canons' choir stalls, Goslar's oldest stained glass picture, Romanesque madonna statues, and Gothic altars complete the exhibit.

Die bedeutendste mittelalterliche Plastik Goslars schuf Hans Witten mit der Pieta in St. Jakobi (1520).
Hans Witten created the pieta at St. Jacob's Church in 1520. It is Goslar's most important medieval sculpture.

St. Jakobi trägt seine Schlagglocke wie einen Ohrring außen am Turm. Diese einzige katholische Innenstadtkirche wurde 1527 als erste in Goslar evangelisch und blieb es bis 1803.
Like an earring the bell adorns the outside of the tower of St. Jacob's Church. Today Goslar's only Catholic church, it became its first Protestant one in 1527 and stayed Protestant until 1803.

sche Steinmetze Wunderwerke in den Stein „zauberten". Zweihundert Jahre nach dem Weggang der Augustiner Chorherren hielt im Jahr 1990 die Gethesmane-Bruderschaft nach der Restaurierung der Klostergebäude Einzug, Niedersachsens einziges evangelisches Männerkloster.

Nichts verrät das schlichte Äußere der **Klosterkirche Grauhof (1711)** von der verschwenderischen barocken Pracht in ihrem Inneren. In den Sommermonaten pilgern Orgelfreunde von nah und fern nach Grauhof, um im Rahmen des „Goslarer Orgelsommers" berühmte Orgelspieler aus Europa zu hören. Anlaß für ihre Konzerte ist die größte noch erhaltene Orgel des mitteldeutschen Orgelbauers Christoph Treutmann von 1737, die für eine Million Mark restauriert wurde.

Hahnenklee, Goslars „Bel etage" wartet mit einer kirchlichen Arabeske auf. Sie legte sich 1908 eine nach dem Vorbild nordischer Stabkirchen erbaute Holzkirche zu, die sich mittlerweile zu einer begehrten Hochzeitskirche entwickelt hat.

A visitor to the city who wanders beyond the old gates will meet with such gems as the ruins of Riechenberg Abbey. The capitals of the pillars supporting the vaults of its 1150 crypt are miracles carved in stone my Lombardic stonemasons. In 1990, twohundred years after the departure of the Augustinian canons, the Brotherhood of Gethsemane, Lower Saxony's only Protestant male order, moved into the restored monastery buildings.

Nothing in the simple exterior of the former 1711 Augustinian abbey at Grauhof tells of the lavish Baroque splendor inside. During the summer months, "Goslar's Summer of Organ Music" draws a pilgrimage of enthusiasts from far and near who want to listen to famous organ players performing on the church's organ of 1737. Recently restored at the expense of a million marks, it is the largest surviving instrument made by the Middle German master organ builder Christoph Treutmann.

Hahnenklee, Goslar's „bel etage", features a wooden church in the Scandinavian tradition. Built in 1908, is has since become a major favourite for churchweddings.

Barocke Pracht entfaltet die Klosterkirche Grauhof hinter einer schlichten Fassade. Beherrschend der Hauptaltar (1717), flankiert von Verkündigungsaltar (links) und Kreuzesaltar (rechts). Am Chorgestühl im Hohen Chor werden Stationen aus dem Leben des Hl. Augustinus und Ordensregeln der Augustiner dargestellt. Die reichgeschnitzte Kanzel im Vordergrund stammt von 1721.

Behind a plain facade the abbey church Grauhof displays an unexpected Baroque splendour. The interior is dominated by the main altar of 1717, flanked by the annunciation altar (left) and the crucifixion altar (right). The carvings of the choir stalls at the high choir show scenes from the life of St. Augustine and illustrate rules of the Augustinian order. The richly carved pulpit in the foreground is dated 1721.

Das **Mönchehaus**, ein 1582 erbautes Ackerbürgerhaus, ist heute ein Zentrum moderner Kunst. Von weither reisen die Besucher an, um die Ausstellungen der Kaiserringträger zu besichtigen. Seit 1978, seit der Verein zur Förderung moderner Kunst in Goslar die Regie des Hauses übernahm, wissen die großen Künstler den mittelalterlichen Rahmen für ihre Arbeiten zu schätzen, ob es nun Victor Vasarely, Joseph Beuys, Max Bill, Richard Serra, Georg Baselitz, Gerhard Richter oder Nam June Paik sind. Bedeutende Installationen von Günther Uecker und Anselm Kiefer sind Dauerleihgaben. Über den Rahmen der Kunstpreisträger hinaus zeigt das Museum das ganze Jahr über Ausstellungen europäischer Grafiker, Maler und Bildhauer.

Built in 1582 as the house of a landed citizen, the Mönchehaus today is a centre of modern art. Many visitors travel long ways in order to see the exhibitions of the Kaiserring recipients. In 1978 the Society for the Advancement of Modern Art in Goslar took over the management of the house, and since then great artists such as Victor Vasarely, Joseph Beuys, Max Bill, Richard Serra, Georg Baselitz, Gerhard Richter, or June Paik have enjoyed the medieval setting to present their work. Famous installations by Günther Uecker and Anselm Kiefer are on permanent loan to the museum. Besides the exhibitions of the Kaiserring recipients, the museum features graphic artists, painters, and sculptors from all over Europe, whether established

Der letzte von Christo verpackte Förderwagen ("Hunt") des Erzbergwerks Rammelsberg im Mönchehaus-Museum - Das reichgeschnitzte Portal des Hauses (1528) - Das Mobile "Rotschwarzer Dreifuß" von Alexander Calder im Skulpturengarten.

At the Mönchehaus museum: "The last ore cart of the Rammelsberg mines" wrapped by Christo -- the richly carved portal of 1528 -- Alexander Calder's mobile "Red and Black Tripod" at the museum's sculpture garden.

Die mittelalterliche Jakobistraße mit dem Mönchehaus (1528), Museum für moderne Kunst.

The medieval Jakobistraße with the Mönchehaus (1528), the museum of modern art.

Unmittelbar hinter dem Bahnhof drängen sich die Sehenswürdigkeiten: Neuwerk, Achtermann, Rosentor. Der Rest des Rosentores noch mit dem alten Wehrgang, davor die von dem Kolumbianer Botero geschaffene Skulptur.

In the immediate vicinity of the railway station, the Neuwerk Church, the Achtermann tower and the Rosentor gate line up like pearls on a string. In the foreground a sculpture by the Colombian artist Botero.

Gegenüber dem Rosentor steht noch sein wuchtiger äußerer Flankierungsturm, der Achtermann. Längst ist er endgültig "entmilitarisiert" und als Aushängeschild in die Anlage des Hotels "Der Achtermann" integriert.

Opposite the Rosentor gate, the former outer flanking tower of the Achtermann has long lost all its military functions and lent its name to the hotel complex into which was integrated.

König unter den touristischen Fotomodellen ist das voluminöse Pärchen mit Stock und Regenschirm am Eingang der Fußgängerzone. Die für seinen Schöpfer Fernando Botero typischen üppigen Körpermaße lassen selbst Molligere schlank erscheinen. Das ist Goslars Willkommensgruß für Touristen und Brautpaare vor dem Ehehafen im benachbarten Standesamt.

„Ein Haus wie aus dem Märchen" schrieb Ricarda Huch über das **Kleine Heilige Kreuz**, und wer dächte da nicht an ein Knusperhäuschen? Über die blauen Schieferdächer des Ensembles schiebt sich der barocke Turmhelm der Frankenberger Kirche. Wirklich: ein Bild wie aus dem Märchen, wären da nicht die Autos auf dem

or still up and coming. The sculpture garden is a charming addition to the house itself.

If picture taking tourists were to choose their favourite motif, that rather stout couple at the beginning of the pedestrian zone opposite the Achtermann probably would turn out the unrivalled number one. Typical for the work of their creator, Fernando Botero, the sheer size of the figures makes even the well rounded tourist look as if having been on a diet for weeks. Such flattery is Goslar's welcome to tourists, and also to couples ready to enter the havens of married life at the neighbouring registry office.

"A house sprung from a fairytale" poet Ricarda Huch once

Ein einmaliges Ensemble am Frankenberger Plan ist das Kleine Heilige Kreuz mit dem Küsterhaus und dem Brunnen, einer modifizierten Nachbildung des Nürnberger Rathaushofbrunnens. - Blumen in der Grünanlage gegenüber der Frankenberger Kirche und an den alten Gebäuden.

One of Goslar's gems: The plaza of the Frankenberger Plan with the Kleines Heiliges Kreuz, the verger's house, and the fountain, modelled after the one in front of the Nuremburg townhall. -- Daffodils at the Frankenberg Church gardens -- Flowers in bloom in pots and boxes adorn the old houses.

Wie ein Blick ins Spielzeugland - der Frankenberger Plan.

Like a look into a miniature world - the Frankenberger Plan

Frankenberger Plan. Dieser Platz hat die Funktion von Zentrum und Begegnungsstätte für die Oberstadt und war einstmals ein kleiner Markt. Die den Bergleuten eng verbundene Oberstadt ist ein Dorado der Gäßchen und idyllischen Winkel mit holprigem Wildpflaster, denen noch keine Fußgängerzone die schmalen Bürgersteige raubte. Ihr ungekrönter Star, die Peterstraße, läßt die Fotografen zwanghaft zur Kamera greifen.

Ehemalige Befestigungsanlagen besitzt die Oberstadt dagegen nur noch in Resten, beispielsweise die sehr geschickt modern überbauten Rudimente des Schmiedeturms am Kloster Frankenberg, die Stadtmauer an der Frankenberger Kirche, die Klauskapelle als Torkapelle und in der Bäringerstraße den Wachtmeisterturm.

Kaiserpfalz, Kirchen, Hospitäler, Gildehäuser, Befestigungsanlagen – sie sind die Perlen in der Goldkette der **Bürgerhäuser**. Was wären diese Perlen ohne das Grundmuster der Wohnhäuser! Hausgestalten unterschiedlichster sozialer Herkunft geben sich an Straßen und

wrote with reference to the Kleines Heiliges Kreuz; and who would not be thinking of a gingerbread house then? If it were not for the parking cars on the Frankenberger Plan, the scene could be that of a fairytale, with the Baroque steeple of the Frankenberg Church peeking out over the bluish slate roofs of this ensemble. The plaza in front serves as the meeting place of the Upper Town and once was a small market in its own right. The Upper Town, closely linked with the miners' past, is a dorado of narrow alleys and idyllic corners with cobblestone pavement where no pedestrian zone has yet devoured the small sidewalks. The uncrowned star among them, the Peterstraße, is the cause for many cases of rampant photomania.

There are only a few remains of the former fortifications left at the Upper Town, for example the ruins of the Schmiedeturm, craftily incorporated into the Frankenberg Monastery, the townwall at the Frankenberg Church, the Klaus Chapel as former gate chapel, and the Wachtmeisterturm (Constable's Tower) at the Bäringerstraße.

Kokett spiegeln sich Kleines Heiliges Kreuz und Küsterhaus im Wasser des Brunnens auf dem Frankenberger Plan. An dem aus dem 14. Jahrhundert stammenden Hospital, das heute Gemeindehaus ist, grüßen die Stifterwappen und das Wappen der Stadt Goslar die Besucher.

The Kleines Heiliges Kreuz and the verger's house are playfully reflected in the waters of the fountain on the Frankenberger Plan. Built in the 14th century, the former hospital today houses the parish rooms. Visitors are greeted by the coats of arms of the founders and of the city of Goslar.

Gassen ein Stelldichein, das Bergmannshäuschen und das Patrizierhaus, das sogar noch eine steinerne Kemenate vorweisen kann, das Hirtenhaus und das Ackerbürgerhaus. Der reiche Handelsherr Hans Siemens stattete das Stammhaus seiner Familie mit kunstvoll gestalteten roten Ziegelgefachen zwischen dunklem Fachwerk aus, der Glockengießermeister Magnus Karsten gegenüber sparte nicht an reichem Schnitzwerk und Inschriften.

Die Armen tragen nur eine bescheidene Holzkette mit ihren Fachwerkbalken, indessen die Schnitzereien der Reichen mit Brillantcolliers wetteifern. Die Last der Jahrhunderte hat, für jedermann sichtbar, so manchen Balken krumm gezogen. Andere Häuser verbergen die Alters-

The imperial palace, the churches, the hospices, the guildhalls, and the fortifications – they all are the pearls in the golden necklace of private houses. For what would they be without this backdrop pattern of the old living quarters? Houses of the most different design and social standing harmonize to create this architectural symphony, from the miner's cottage to the patrician villa with a stone ground floor, from the shepherd's cot to the house of the landed citizen. At the mansion of the wealthy merchant Hans Siemens the squares of the dark timber-frame were filled in with red brick, while across the street, the residence of the master bellfounder Magnus Karsten was lavishly decorated with carvings and inscriptions.

Vom stattlichen Vititor in der Bäringerstraße ist nicht mehr viel übriggeblieben. Im „Wachtmeisterturm" hat man eine schön geschnitzte Tür aus einem Bürgerhaus eingebaut.

Little is left of the once stately Vititor gate. Its "Wachtmeisterturm" today is adorned by a beautifully carved door from a patrician house.

Das Stammhaus der Familie Siemens (1693) ist ein Prachtbau. Ein Prunkbau ist auch sein Brauhaus, in dem Goslars Exportschlager, das Gose-Bier, gebraut wurde.

The ancestral home of the Siemens family is a stately mansion of 1693.

beschwerden unter dem blauen Fischschuppenkleid aus Schiefer.

Das Mittelalter war die hohe Zeit der Holzschnitzer, deren halbe Sonnenräder, wilde Männer, Eierketten und Lebensbäume dem Betrachter aus dem Computerzeitalter wie geheimnisvolle Kürzel alten Brauchtums grüßen. Und welches Arsenal hatte man seinerzeit zur Abwehr des Bösen vorrätig mit den „Bleekern", den Schreckgesichtern mit der überdimensionierten Zunge, mit Zauberknoten, Sechsstern und Pentagramm.

Manchmal gleichen die Hausinschriften im Verein mit den Wappen und Marken der Bauherrschaft einem Lesebuch, in dem man sowohl Stadtgeschichte als auch Familiengeschichte erforschen kann. Feministinnen dürfen aufjuchzen, denn öfters wird der Name der Hausfrau neben dem des Hausherrn in Holz festgehalten, weil „sie" seinerzeit eine ganze Menge zu sagen hatte. Wer allerdings damals auf sich hielt, bevorzugte lateinische Inschriften, und diese Bildungsbeflissenheit setzt heute gewisse Barrieren. Die Gosla-

The half-timbered houses of the poor wear their wooden decor of simply carved beams with pride, while the carvings of the rich compete with each other like diamond necklaces. Visible to all, the burden of centuries has bent many a beam. Other houses hide the pangs of old age behind a facade of overlapping slate shingles.

The Middle Ages were the heydays of the wood-carvers. Their designs of palmettes, wild men, egg-shaped chains, and trees of life seem like secret runes of old to us children of the computer age. For little do we know of the defenses against evil that our ancestors once wielded, for example the "Bleekers", those terrifying faces with their oversized tongues, or the magic knots, the hexagrams and pentagrams.

At times the inscriptions, the coats of arms, and the trademarks of the builders combine into an open book of family and town history. The feminists of today have reason to rejoice, for more than once the name of the woman of the house is named right along with that of her husband. After all, "she" did have

Die Mietzekatze paßt wie bestellt ins Bild vom Knusperhäuschen.

As if it had been waiting for it, the kitten picked the right time to appear before the "gingerbread house".

Im „Hirtenhaus" (1582) wohnte früher der städtische Hirte. Bis nach 1945 wurden Kuh- und Ziegenherden noch durch die Stadt getrieben.

The "Hirtenhaus" (herdsman's cottage) of 1582 once was the home of the city's official herdsman. Even past 1945, cow and goat herds were still driven through town.

rer von einst müssen zudem fromme Leute gewesen sein, denn in jeder zweiten Inschrift wird Gott um Beistand gebeten. Was wiederum angesichts des geschnitzten heidnischen Abwehrzaubers zumindest den Zipfel des Verdachts aufkommen läßt, sie seien so ein bißchen nach dem Motto „Doppelt genäht hält besser" vorgegangen.

Moderne Bauherren verblassen vor Neid weniger vor dem Reichtum ihrer Kollegen aus früheren Jahrhunderten denn vor den an Hexerei grenzenden Bauzeiten. Nicht nur an einem Haus kann man nachlesen, an welchem Tag es errichtet wurde. Zum Beispiel in der Glockengießerstraße 30: „Anno domini 1567, den 4. Aprilis". Nach umfangreichen Vorarbeiten war das für die Zimmermeister möglich.

Wachen Geistes und gutbeschuht müssen die Touristen sein, wollen sie reiche Erinnerungsbeute nach Hause tragen. Auf dem Marktplatz haben die Stadtväter den Besucherinnen mit Bleistiftabsätzen noch einen einigermaßen gehfreundlichen Pflasterteppich ausgerollt. Im „lupenreinen" Mittelalter der Jakobi- oder Peterstraße

80

the say in the house in those days. Yet, our eagerness to learn is severly curtailed by the fact that many of our forbears, conscious of their social status, used Latin for their inscriptions. The Goslarians of those days must also have been a pious people, for every second inscription invokes the help of the Lord. Since this hardly agrees with the heathen symbols used to defy evil spirits, one can't help but assume that they followed the old motto of "better safe than sorry."

It is not so much the wealth of their forbears that makes today's building clients pale of envy but a speed of construction short of witchcraft. On more than one house one cannot only read the year but also the day of its erection. A good example is the house at the Glockengießerstraße 30: "Built in the Year of the Lord 1567 on the Fourth of April." After extensive preparations the master carpenters indeed were able of such a feat.

A keen mind and suitable footwear are a must for the Goslar tourists if they want to take home a rich harvest of memories. Thanks to the city fathers, the marketplace has

Fachwerkvariationen am Schuhhof, Goslars ältester Platzanlage.

Variations of timber frame work at the Schuhhof, Goslar's oldest plaza.

Die Peterstraße mit ihren schmucken und blumengeschmückten Fachwerkhäusern zählt zu Goslars schönsten Straßen. Vorn rechts das "Haus mit dem Kürbis".

Some decorated with flowers, the neat half-timbered houses of the Peterstraße make this street one of Goslar's finest. To the right in the foreground the "House with the Pumpkin".

sieht man sie dagegen wie Störche übers „Wildpflaster" steigen, das man früher bieder „Kopfsteinpflaster" nannte. Meinte nicht Heine schon, das Goslarer Pflaster sei holperiger als Berliner Hexameter?

Wer hier entlangbalanciert, taucht ein ins Mittelalter, das nichts vom monotonen Schachbrettmuster moderner Straßen ahnte. Seine Gassen krümmen sich, verlieren sich im Winkel, und unvermutet schiebt sich ein Haus in den Straßenraum – mittelalterliches „Hinweisschild" auf die Vorfahrt der anderen Seite.

Zu Goslars Schätzen schließlich gehören die privaten grünen Oasen, die niemand hinter den geschlossenen Häuserzeilen vermutet, öffentlichen Grünanlagen inmitten der Altstadt und die Phalanx der Bäume vom Baby bis zu 400 Jahre alten Methusalems. Grün, das im Süden der Stadt sorgsam im Dreiklang Stadt – Wiesen – Wald gehütet wird.

a pavement still reasonably suitable for ladies with stiletto heels. But once they meet with the true Middle Ages at the Jakobistraße or Peterstraße, those ladies are stalking along the "irregular pavement" (a new term for the old cobblestones) like storks through a salad bed. Wasn't the poet Heinrich Heine the first to complain that Goslar's pavements in their irregularity were worse than a Berlin hexameter?

Anyone balancing along these streets is taken on a journey to the Middle Ages that knew nothing of the monotonous grid design of our modern days. Lanes and alleys wind along to lose themselves in quiet, picturesque corners, and at times a house simply juts out into the street like a medieval traffic signal announcing the right of way of oncoming vehicles..
Not to be forgotten among the treasures of Goslar are the many private spots of green that no one expects behind the unbroken rows of houses, the public parks in the middle of the Old Town, and the phalanx of trees from the tiny yearlings to the ancient fourhundred years old Methuselas.

Die Stadtbücherei verfügt im Patrizierhaus Marktstraße 1 (1526) über Räume mit einzigartigem Flair. Bei der Restaurierung wurde das zweite Haus farblich abgesetzt.

The city library resides in rooms of a singular atmosphere at the patrician house at Marktstraße 1, built in 1526. When the buildings were restored, the second one received a slightly different colour.

Stelldichein köstlicher kleiner Hausgestalten am Liebfrauenberg zu Füßen der Kaiserpfalz.

Little houses huddle at the Liebfrauenberg at the foot of the Imperial Palace.

Das Goslarer Museum

Eine Schatzkammer ist das städtische Museum. Stadtgeschichte in ihrem Facettenreichtum, glänzend präsentiert, "liest" sich spannend. Die Kirchenkunst-Ausstellung mit ihrem meditativen Charakter steht im Mittelpunkt.

Einmalige Kostbarkeiten aus dem Mittelalter geben sich hier ein Stelldichein: Das bedeutende Goslarer Evangeliar (1240), intensiv leuchtende Glasfenster, unter ihnen die älteste in Goslar erhaltene Scheibe von 1240 mit der Geburt Christi, der geheimnis-

The Goslar Museum

The city museum is a treasure chest filled to its very brim. Viewing the splendid presentations of the city's history is like reading a fascinating book of which the exhibits of religious art with their meditative character are the central parts.

Many outstanding and unique treasures from the Middle Ages have been gathered here: among them are the famous Goslar Bible (1240) and impressive stained glass windows with intensive colours, including the oldest one in Goslar (about 1240), showing

Goslarer Evangeliar (1240):
Links und rechts Initialseiten des Markus- und Johannes-Evangeliums, in der Mitte eine Bildseite des Lukas-Evangeliums.

Goslar Bible (1240):
To the left and right are initial pages of St. Mark's and St. John's Gospel, at the centre a picture page from the Gospel according to St. Luke.

Die Glasscheibe aus dem Dom ist das älteste Goslarer Fenster.

This stained glass window from the Goslar cathedral is the oldest window in Goslar.

umwobene "goldene Altar", der Krodoaltar (erste Hälfte des 12. Jahrhunderts), riesige Wandteppiche, einst die Rücklaken des Chorgestühls im Dom. Mit den Jahrhunderten durchschreitet der Besucher Welten der Darstellung und des Empfindens: Von strenger Hoheit die Madonna mit dem Kind auf dem Thron (1230) und von wundersamer Innigkeit ein Lindenholzrelief, auf dem Maria Magdalena und Johannes Maria trösten (um 1460).

Überlebensgroß beherrschen die Figuren der Kreuzigungsgruppe die Stirnseite des Domraums. Sie standen in dem 1820 abgebrochenen Dom auf einem Kielbogen über dem Lettner. Wer die Räume betritt, ahnt etwas von der Schönheit des Domes. Gleichzeitig kann er in einem Sonderraum anhand des Petri-Altars einen Blick hinter die Kulissen der Restaurierungstechniken und somit in die Moderne werfen.

Ob Ur- und Frühgeschichte, Münzwesen, Stadtbefestigung oder Fachwerkbau mit spätgotischen Wandmalereien aus einem abgebrannten Haus: Der Museumsbesuch gleicht einer Entdeckungsreise.

the birth of Jesus Christ. There are the still mysterious "golden altar", the Krodo altar (first half of the 12th century), and huge tapestries, once the back of the choir stalls of the cathedral. Passing through the centuries, visitors also pass through different worlds of feeling and expression: here the reserved majesty of Madonna and Child on the throne (1230), there a linden wood relief of profound intimacy with Mary Magdalena and John consoling Mary (about 1460).

Larger than life, the statues of the crucifixion group dominate the end wall of the cathedral room. Before the Goslar cathedral was demolished in 1820, they had their place on an ogee arch above the choir screen. They give the visitor at least a vague idea of the lost beauty of the cathedral. In a special separate room the visitor cannot only view the Petri-Altar but also have a glimpse at modern restoring techniques.

Whether you are looking at prehistory or the early days, the mint, the town fortifications or a half-timbered house with the late Gothic murals saved burned ruins, a visit to the museum is always an adventure.

Goslars erster Kaiserringträger, der englische Bildhauer Henry Moore, war 1974 fasziniert von der Kreuzigungsgruppe aus dem Dom. Hundert Jahre zuvor hatte der Kunsthistoriker Mitthoff noch geschrieben: "Mehrere colossale Holzfiguren ohne Kunstwerth". Die Figuren sind bewußt auf die Betrachtung aus großer Entfernung angelegt. (Restauratoren entdeckten 1931 im Kopf der Christusfigur einen Pergamentstreifen mit dem Entstehungsjahr der Figuren: 1520)

In 1974 the English sculptor Henry Moore, the first artist to receive Goslar's modern art reward "Kaiserring", was fascinated by the crucifixion group from the old Goslar cathedral. Only a hundred years before, the art critic Mithoff wrote about this same group: "Several rather colossal wooden figures without any artistic value". The statues have been consciously designed to be seen from afar. (In 1931 restorers found a piece of parchment in the head of the Jesus figure naming the year of its making: 1520)

Die im Museum aufbewahrte Bergkanne (1477) gehört in ihrer Eleganz und Einheitlichkeit zu den kostbarsten Silberarbeiten der deutschen Gotik. Die vom Bergbau- und Hüttenunternehmer Thurzo dem Rat geschenkte Kanne ist eine Symbol für die enge Verbindung zwischen der Stadt Goslar und ihrem Schicksalsberg, dem Rammelsberg. So zieren den Deckelrand zwei Bergleute mit Haspel, ein Erzwagen mit Pferd und Reiter und ein Mann mit Schaufel. Halbplastische Bergmusikanten lugen aus dem Laub der Buckelzone.

With its elegance and artistic unity, the Bergkanne (1477), kept at the city museum today, is among the most precious works of Gothic silversmiths. Once presented to the city council as a gift by a Mr Thurzo, a wealthy owner of mines and smelters, this pitcher is a living symbol of the close ties between the city of Goslar and its mountain of fate, the Rammelsberg. The pitcher's lid is adorned by the figures of two miners with windlasses, an ore cart with horse and rider, and a man with a shovel. Musicians peek out from the leaves at the rounded belly.

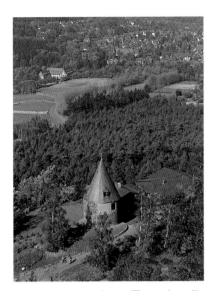

Der Maltermeister Turm ist die älteste deutsche Tagesanlage eines Bergwerks. Von hier hat man einen umfassenden Blick auf Goslar.

The Maltermeister Turm is Germany's oldest surface installation at a mine. From here the eyes gaze far and wide over the city of Goslar.

Im Bergwerk

Als die tausendjährige Geschichte des Erzbergwerks Rammelsberg am 30. Juni 1988 endete, standen den Bergleuten Tränen in den Augen. Es ging ihnen um mehr noch als um ihre Arbeitsplätze. Für die Stadt Goslar aber ging es um Erhalt oder Nichterhalt dieses einmaligen Industriedenkmals. In konzertierten Aktionen von Denkmalpflege, Bürgern, Stadt, Land und Bund wurden die Weichen für das kostspielige Projekt auf Grün gestellt. Die Aufnahme in die Liste des UNESCO-Weltkulturerbes bestätigte die Richtigkeit dieser Entscheidung. Sie wird auch bestätigt durch den Part, den der Rammelsberg als dezentrales Projekt der Expo 2000 unter dem Titel "Expo on the rocks" übernimmt.

Schätzungsweise 30 Millionen Tonnen Erze sind seit dem offiziellen Beginn des Bergwerks im Jahr 968 gefördert worden. Anfänge des Bergbaus hat es jedoch am Rammelsberg schon im 3. Jahrhundert nach Christus gegeben.

Das Bergwerk, im Originalzustand erhalten, ist ein Technikdenkmal der Superlative:

At the Mines

When more of a thousand years of mining ended at the Rammelsberg Mines on June 30th, 1988, miners were weeping not only for their jobs. For Goslar it was a do or die issue to retain this unique industrial monument. And in a combined effort of the curators of monuments, the town council, the State of Lower Saxony, the Federal government, and last but certainly not least Goslar's citizens, the expensive project was brought on its way. The UNESCO's decision to make the mines a listed site of world cultural heritage thoroughly underlines the reasonability of these efforts. They are further justified by the role the Rammelsberg mines will play as a decentralised project of the Expo 2000: "Expo on the rocks".

It has been estimated that some 30 million tons of ore have been extracted from the mines since they officially opened in 968. But the Rammelsberg was mined as early as in the 3rd century of our time.

Retained in their original condition, the mines are a technological monument of

Ein Interregio ist die Gruben-bahn nicht, dafür vermittelt sie den Besuchern aber hautnah die Welt der Bergleute.

The mine train certainly isn't an intercity express train, but it does take the visitors on a hands on tour of the miners' world.

Eine auch architektonisch be-wundernswerte Leistung ist die Erzaufbereitung.

Beyond its functionality, the ore treatment plant is also an architectural masterpiece.

Der Rathstiefste Stollen (12. Jhdt.) zählt zu den ältesten Stollen in Deutschland, das Feuergezäher Gewölbe (13. Jhdt.) ist gar der älteste, ge-mauerte Grubenraum Euro-pas und der Maltermeister Turm das älteste Taggebäude des deutschen Bergbaus. Die Aufbereitungsanlagen, die die technischen Aufgaben des Betriebsablaufes mit beein-druckender künstlerischer Ge-staltung verbinden, sind eine herausragende architektoni-sche Leistung. Einer der wohl bedeutendsten Industriebau-meister des 20. Jahrhunderts, Fritz Schupp (1896-1974), hat sie geschaffen.

Tausend Jahre Bergbau "zum Anfassen" im Besucherberg-werk. Stollen, Schächte, wuchtige Kehrräder, die ei-nem Kirchenschiff gleichende Waschkaue, wären da nicht die Kleiderkörbe an der Dek-ke, in denen die Bergleute ihre Kleidung verstauten. Das ist kein geschniegeltes Muse-um, in dem täglich Staub ge-wischt wird. Hier und da tropft das Wasser von der Decke auf den Schutzhelm, und die Grubenbahn rüttelt die Fahr-gäste genau wie früher die Bergleute durcheinander: Authentizität heißt das Leit-motiv. Hier werden montan-

superlatives: The Rathstiefste Stollen (12th century) is among the oldest horizontal drifts in Germany, the Feuergezäher Gewölbe (13th century) once housed giant waterwheels and is the oldest brick-lined underground chamber found in a mine in Europe, while the Maltermeister Turm is the oldest surface building in German mining history. Com-bining technological needs and functions with impressively artistic design, the ore treat-ment plant is an unrivalled architectural marvel, created by Fritz Schupp (1896-1974), one of the greatest industrial architects of the 20th century.

The show-mine provides a hands-on experience of more than a thousand years of min-ing: the drifts and shafts, the massive driving- and water-wheels, the miners' changing room and washery, more like the nave of a church if it were not for the baskets under the roof holding the miners' clothes. This is no fancy mu-seum where exhibits are cleaned and dusted daily. There is still water dripping from the ceiling onto the visi-tor's safety helmet, and the underground train still shakes up its passengers as it once did the miners: Authenticity

technische und Sozialgeschichte an dem Ort aufgezeigt, an dem sie sich ereignet haben, und die Erhaltung von Gebrauchsspuren ist eine Selbstverständlichkeit.

Denn das Bergwerk selbst ist ein beeindruckendes riesiges Exponat, das die Besucher in die Welt über und unter Tage führt. Es umschließt das noch im Aufbau befindliche Bergbaumuseum, das das Denkmal Bergwerk "zum Sprechen" bringen soll. Hier wie mit der Grubenbahn, dem Grubenjeep, dem Förderkorb oder zu Fuß erkunden die Besucher die Arbeitsgeschichte des Rammelsberges, die ein lebendiges Dokument des Bergbaus ist. Der Blick wird über Schächte und Stollen von der Technikgeschichte hinausgelenkt auf Wirtschafts- und Kulturgeschichte. Und somit ersteht fast wie von selbst das Bild des Bergbaus als einem Motor gesellschaftlicher und politischer Entwicklung. Der Rammelsberg hat Goslars Geschichte, hat die Altstadt mit ihren prächtigen Bauten ebenso geprägt wie seine unmittelbare landschaftliche Umgebung mit ihren schroffen Halden und nur karger Vegetation, dem Herzberger Teich oder den Erzabfuhrwegen.

is the guiding motif here. Mining history and social history are shown where it once happened. So preserving the traces of past wear and tear is a logical consequence.

The entire mine today is just one impressive and vast exhibit introducing the visitor as much to the world above as to the world below the surface. All the activities in the developing museum serve just one single purpose: making the mine "talk". Whether by mine train or by jeep, by mine cage or just on foot, the visitors are challenged to explore the working history of the Rammelsberg, this great living document of mines and mining. Almost automatically the eye begins to roam beyond the history of the technology of shafts and drifts and perceives the many additional facets of economic and social history. Thus the mine as the crucial driving force behind any social and political development becomes visible. The Rammelsberg has determined the course of Goslar's history and the shape of the old town as much as its immediate surrounding landscape with the rough slagheaps and their poor vegetation, the Herzberg pond or the ore roads.

Auch der Förderturm gehört zu den Denkmälern des Bergwerks.
The winding tower, too, is part of the mine's historical monument.

Rechts: Giganten gleichen die Kehrräder untertage.
Right: Giants of another age, the waterwheels underground in the mines.

Seite 94/95: Der Marktplatz in weihnachtlicher Verzauberung.
Page 94/95: A dream of Christmas at Goslar's marketplace.

Seite 96: Linde am Schuhhof im Schneekleid.
Page 96: The linden tree at the Schuhhof with an enchanting cover of snow.